# CAKES
## AND
## COOKIES

**imagine** THAT!™

Imagine That! is an imprint of Top That! Publishing plc,
Tide Mill Way, Woodbridge, Suffolk, IP12 IAP, UK
www.topthatpublishing.com

# Contents

# Cookies continued

# Sweets

# Cooking Equipment

Before you begin to get creative in the kitchen, it's a good idea to take a look through the drawers and cupboards to make sure you know where all the cooking equipment is kept.

• To complete the recipes in this book, you will need to use a selection of everyday cooking equipment and utensils, such as mixing bowls, saucepans, a sieve, knives, spoons and forks and a chopping board.

• Of course, you'll need to weigh and measure the ingredients, so you'll need a measuring jug and some kitchen scales too.

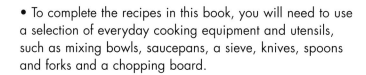

• Some of the recipes tell you to use a whisk. Ask an adult to help you use an electric whisk, or you can use a balloon whisk yourself – you'll just have to work extra hard!

• To make some of the cakes, cookies and sweets, you'll need to use the correct-sized cake tins or other special equipment. These items (and others that you may not have to hand) are listed at the start of each recipe.

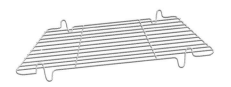

# Safety and Hygiene

It is important to take care in the kitchen as there are lots of potential hazards and hygiene risks.

 • **Take Note!**
**Whenever you see**
**the warning triangle**
**you will need**
**adult supervision.**

• Before starting any cooking always wash your hands.

• Cover any cuts with a plaster.

• Wear an apron to protect your clothes.

• Always make sure that all the equipment you use is clean.

• If you need to use a sharp knife to cut up something hard, ask an adult to help you. Always use a chopping board.

• Remember that trays in the oven and pans on the cooker can get very hot. **Always ask an adult to turn on the oven and to get things in and out of the oven for you.**

• Always ask an adult for help if you are using anything electrical – like an electric whisk.

• Be careful when heating anything in a pan on top of the cooker. Keep the handle turned to one side to avoid accidentally knocking the pan.

• Keep your pets out of the kitchen while cooking.

# Getting Started

Making your own biscuits, cakes and sweets is great fun and really quite easy. Best of all, everyone will enjoy what you create!

## Measuring:

Use scales to weigh exactly how much of each ingredient you need or use a measuring jug to measure liquids.

## Mixing:

Use a spoon, balloon whisk or electric hand whisk to mix the ingredients together.

## Different ideas:

Decorate your cakes and biscuits with flavoured or coloured icing, and then add chocolate drops, sweets or sugar strands.

## Different shapes:

Cookie cutters come in lots of different shapes and sizes, and can be bought from most supermarkets. If you don't have any cookie cutters of your own, carefully use a knife to cut out the shapes you want.

## Creating recipes:

Once you've made a recipe in this book a few times, think about whether you could make your own version. Why not mix some chocolate chips into the Yummy Flapjacks mixture or add desiccated coconut to the Crunchy Cookies? This way you can start to make up your own recipes. Try to think up names for the things you create!

Read through each recipe to make sure you've got all the ingredients that you need before you start.

Always ask an adult for help if you are not sure about anything.

# Marble-ous Cake

This marble cake looks really impressive and it's easy to make!

# Marble-ous Cake

**1** Put the cake tin onto a sheet of greaseproof paper and draw around it. Cut out the circle of paper. Use a paper towel to grease the tin with a little soft margarine, and then put the circle of greaseproof paper inside the tin. Grease the paper.

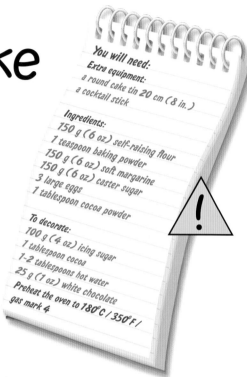

You will need:

Extra equipment:
a round cake tin 20 cm (8 in.)
a cocktail stick

Ingredients:
150 g (6 oz) self-raising flour
1 teaspoon baking powder
150 g (6 oz) soft margarine
150 g (6 oz) caster sugar
3 large eggs
1 tablespoon cocoa powder

To decorate:
100 g (4 oz) icing sugar
1 tablespoon cocoa
1-2 tablespoons hot water
25 g (1 oz) white chocolate
Preheat the oven to 180°C / 350°F /
gas mark 4

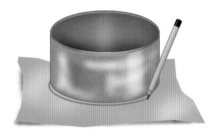

**2** Sift the flower and baking powder into a mixing bowl.

**4** Put half the mixture into another bowl, and then sift the cocoa on top of it. Mix it in well.

**3** Add the margarine, sugar and eggs. Beat everything together with a wooden spoon until completely mixed.

8

**5** Put alternate spoonfuls of the different-coloured mixtures into the tin. Swirl them together a little, and then smooth the top. Put the tin in the centre of the oven and bake for 40–50 minutes.

**6** Take the cake out of the oven and leave it in the tin for five minutes. Turn it out onto a wire rack, peel off the greaseproof paper, turn it over and leave it to cool.

## Decorating the Cake

**1** Before you start to decorate the cake, ask an adult to help you cut it in half as shown.

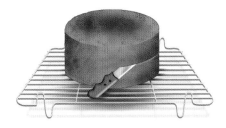

**2** Sift the icing sugar and cocoa into a bowl. Add the hot water, and stir the ingredients together until the mixture is completely chocolate brown.

**3** Spread some icing on the one half of the cake, and then place the other half on top to sandwich the icing. Pour the rest of the icing over the top of the cake and neatly spread it to the edges.

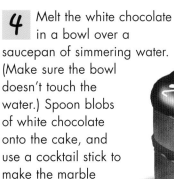

**4** Melt the white chocolate in a bowl over a saucepan of simmering water. (Make sure the bowl doesn't touch the water.) Spoon blobs of white chocolate onto the cake, and use a cocktail stick to make the marble effect shown.

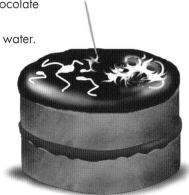

9

# Spiral Cake

This swirly Spiral Cake makes a perfect tea time treat

# Spiral Cake

**1** Put the tin on a sheet of greaseproof paper and draw around it, leaving an edge of 2.5 cm (1 in.). Cut out the paper shape, and make a slit at each corner. Grease the tin with some soft margarine. Now fit the paper into the tin, folding in the edges. Finally, grease the paper.

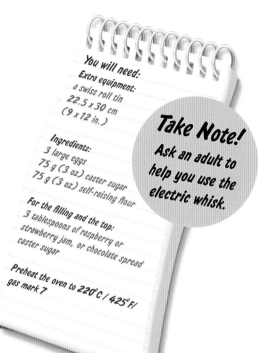

**You will need:**

Extra equipment:
a swiss roll tin
22.5 x 30 cm
(9 x 12 in.)

Ingredients:
3 large eggs
75 g (3 oz) caster sugar
75 g (3 oz) self-raising flour

For the filling and the top:
3 tablespoons of raspberry or
strawberry jam, or chocolate spread
caster sugar

Preheat the oven to 220°C / 425°F/
gas mark 7

**Take Note!** Ask an adult to help you use the electric whisk.

**2** Break the eggs into a large bowl. Add the sugar, and whisk for a few minutes until the mixture is very light and creamy.

**3** Hold the sieve above the bowl and sift the flour into the mixture. Use a tablespoon to stir in the flour, using a gentle figure-of-eight movement – you don't want to knock out the air you've just whisked in!

**4** Put the mixture into the tin, and then smooth the top with the back of a tablespoon. Bake for 7–10 minutes, until the edges have shrunk slightly away from the tin. Leave the cake to cool in the tin for 1–2 minutes.

11

**5** Lay out another sheet of greaseproof paper, and sprinkle caster sugar all over it. Whilst the cake is still warm, turn it out onto the paper. Trim off the edges with a knife.

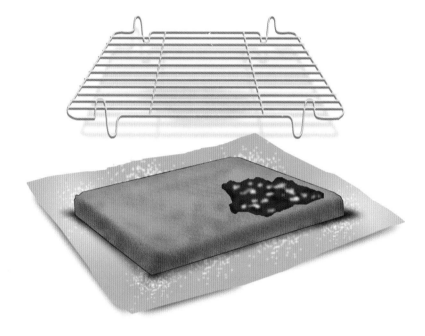

**6** Spread the cake with jam or chocolate spread. Now roll the cake quite tightly, using the greaseproof paper to help you. Sprinkle some caster sugar over the cake to finish.

### Top Tip
Stand the jar of jam or chocolate spread in hot water for about 10 minutes before you need to use it. This will make it easier to spread.

# Easy Christmas Cake

Make this festive treat for your whole family to enjoy

# Easy Christmas Cake

**1** Grease the loaf tin with a little margarine. Put the margarine, egg and pear and apple spread (or honey) in a bowl and mix them together until they're light and creamy.

**2** Sift the flour into the bowl, and mix it in gently. Add the mincemeat and mix well. Then add enough orange juice to make a soft mixture.

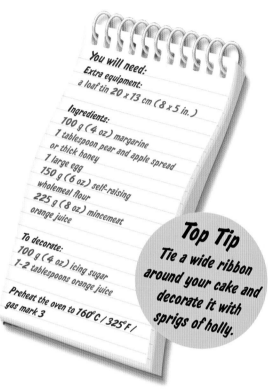

You will need:
Extra equipment:
a loaf tin 20 x 13 cm (8 x 5 in.)

Ingredients:
100 g (4 oz) margarine
1 tablespoon pear and apple spread
or thick honey
1 large egg
150 g (6 oz) self-raising
wholemeal flour
225 g (8 oz) mincemeat
orange juice

To decorate:
100 g (4 oz) icing sugar
1-2 tablespoons orange juice

Preheat the oven to 160°C / 325°F /
gas mark 3

**Top Tip**
Tie a wide ribbon around your cake and decorate it with sprigs of holly.

**3** Put the mixture into the tin, smoothing the top with the spoon. Bake for 40 minutes, until it is golden brown.

**4** Leave the cake in the tin for five minutes, and then turn it out onto a wire rack to cool.

**5** Sieve the icing sugar into a bowl, and mix in enough orange juice to make a thick paste. Spoon the mixture over the cake, letting it run down the sides.

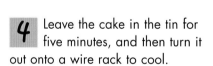

# Treasure Chest Cake

Perfect for pirates, this cake is crammed full of yummy sweets!

# Treasure Chest Cake

**1** Grease the inside of the tin with some soft margarine. Cut a piece of greaseproof paper large enough to fit inside the tin. Slit the corners of the paper and fit it in the tin. Lightly grease the paper.

**2** Put the margarine and sugar into a bowl and beat them together until the mixture is light and fluffy. Add the eggs one at a time, beating each one in well.

**4** Spoon the mixture into the tin, and smooth the top. Bake the cake for about 25 minutes until it is golden. Leave it to cool in the tin for five minutes before turning it out onto a wire rack to cool. Peel off the greaseproof paper.

**3** Sift the flour and cocoa into the mixture, and gently stir them in with a tablespoon. Add a little water to make the mixture soft.

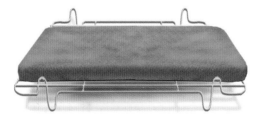

**You will need:**

Extra equipment:
a shallow baking tin
35 x 23 cm (14 x 9 in.)
8 plastic cocktail sticks

Ingredients:
225 g (8 oz) soft margarine
225 g (8 oz) caster sugar
4 eggs
225 g (8 oz) self-raising flour
25 g (1 oz) cocoa
1-2 tablespoons water

Preheat the oven to 190°C / 375°F / gas mark 5

**To decorate:**
a large jar of chocolate spread
coloured chocolate drops
gold-covered chocolate money
or foil-covered sweets

**5** When the cake is cool, cut it into three equal-sized rectangles. The first piece will form the base of the chest and the second piece will be the lid. Cut a rectangle out of the centre of the third piece, to make the sides of the chest.

**6** Spread a little chocolate spread around the edge of the base. Carefully put the cut-out border on top to make a chest shape. Cover the outside and the edges of the chest with chocolate spread, and stick on the coloured chocolate drops. Cover the outside of the lid with the spread and decorate it with chocolate drops. Now put all the pieces of the cake into a cool place for at least an hour.

**7** Fill the chest with gold-covered chocolate coins or sweets. Push the cocktail sticks halfway into the back edge of the chest. Carefully secure the lid onto the sticks, tilting it open at the front.

**Top Tip**
Put the jar of chocolate spread in a warm place one hour before you need to use it.

17

# Brilliant Buns

Use lots of brightly coloured icing to decorate these brilliant buns!

# Brilliant Buns

**1** Put the paper bun cases in the bun case baking tray. Sift the flour into a bowl.

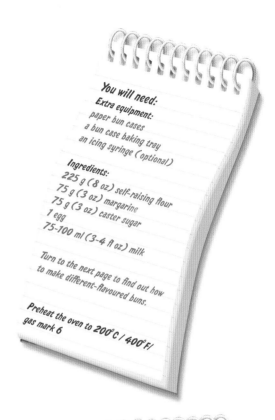

You will need:
Extra equipment:
paper bun cases
a bun case baking tray
an icing syringe (optional)

Ingredients:
225 g (8 oz) self-raising flour
75 g (3 oz) margarine
75 g (3 oz) caster sugar
1 egg
75-100 ml (3-4 fl oz) milk

Turn to the next page to find out how to make different-flavoured buns.

Preheat the oven to 200°C / 400°F/ gas mark 6

**2** Put the margarine in the bowl. Use the tips of your fingers to rub the margarine and flour together until the mixture becomes crumbly.

**3** Add the sugar and mix it in. Now stir in the egg. Finally, add enough milk to make the mixture creamy.

**4** Put spoonfuls of the mixture into the paper cases. Bake the buns for 10–15 minutes, until they are golden brown, then leave them to cool on a wire rack.

| To decorate: | |
|---|---|
| for water icing: | for royal icing: |
| 100 g (4 oz) icing sugar | 100 g (4 oz) icing sugar |
| 1-2 tablespoons of water | 1 egg white |
| food colouring | food colouring |

# Decorating the Buns

**1** Cover the buns with water icing. Here's how to make it! Sift the icing sugar into a bowl. Add 1–2 tablespoons of hot water and mix until you have a smooth thick paste. Add one or two drops of food colouring if you want coloured icing.

To make chocolate icing, add one teaspoon of cocoa powder to the icing sugar before sifting. To make lemon icing, add 1–2 tablespoons of lemon juice instead of hot water.

You can decorate your buns with sugar sprinkles, silver balls or sweets. Once the water icing has set, why not pipe decorations with royal icing?

**2** To make royal icing, beat an egg white in a small bowl. Sift the icing sugar into the bowl. Beat the mixture until the icing becomes smooth and thick. Add a drop of food colouring if you wish. Spoon the icing into an icing syringe and carefully pipe your decoration onto the buns. Leave the icing to set.

**Top Tip**
*Decorate your buns with sugared diamonds, sugar sprinkles, silver balls or small sweets!*

# Variations

## Chocolate Chip Buns

Sift 25 g (1 oz) cocoa into the bowl with the flour. Mix in a handful of chocolate chips. When the buns are cooked and cooled, cover them with chocolate water icing (see method above).

## Coconut Buns

Add 50 g (2 oz) desiccated coconut to the mixture with the sugar. When the buns are cooked, top them with lemon water icing (see method above) and sprinkle them with more coconut.

## Cherry Buns

Add 100 g (4 oz) chopped glacé cherries to the mixture with the sugar. When the buns are cooked, cover them with lemon water icing (see method above) and top each bun with half a glacé cherry.

# Lemon Crystal Buns

These scrumptious lemony buns have a sugar crystal coating

# Lemon Crystal Buns

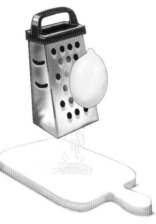

You will need:
Extra equipment:
paper bun cases
a bun case baking tray

Ingredients:
1 lemon
175 g (6 oz) self-raising flour
1 teaspoon baking powder
100 g (4 oz) soft margarine
100 g (4 oz) caster sugar
2 eggs

For the topping:
100 g (4 oz) demerara sugar
juice of 1 lemon

Preheat the oven to 200°C / 400°F/ gas mark 6

**1** Put the paper cases in the bun case baking tray. Ask an adult to help you grate the rind from the lemon, but be careful not to grate any of the white pith. Cut the lemon in half and squeeze the juice into a bowl.

**2** Sift the flour and baking powder into a bowl. Add the margarine, sugar, eggs and grated lemon rind to the bowl, and mix everything together.

**4** While the buns are cooking, make the topping by putting the demerara sugar into the bowl with the lemon juice. Mix them together well.

**5** When the buns are cooked, put them onto a wire rack. While they are still warm, spoon a little of the topping over each one. Leave them to cool.

**3** Spoon the mixture into the paper cases, and bake the buns for 12–15 minutes, until they are golden brown.

# Crackle Cakes

Use cornflakes or crisped rice to make these little cakes crackle!

# Crackle Cakes

**1** Put the sugar, butter, cocoa and golden syrup or honey into a pan over a low heat. Stir until the ingredients have melted.

You will need:
Extra equipment:
paper cake cases

Ingredients:
25 g (1 oz) sugar
25 g (1 oz) butter
2 tablespoons cocoa
1 tablespoon golden syrup or honey
25 g (1 oz) cornflakes

To decorate:
coloured chocolate drops

**Top Tip**
Use crisped rice instead of cornflakes if you prefer.

**2** Stir the cornflakes into the mixture until they are completely coated.

**3** Spoon a little of the mixture into each of the paper cases. Top each with a coloured chocolate drop and leave them to set.

# Healthy Carrot Cake

This cake is packed with carrots to help you see in the dark!

# Healthy Carrot Cake

**1** Put the tin on a sheet of greaseproof paper. Draw around it and cut out the shape. Grease the tin with a little margarine. Put the greaseproof paper inside.

**2** Sift the flour and baking powder into a bowl. Add the sugar, nuts, raisins and carrots and stir them together well.

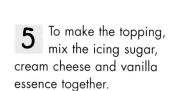

**3** Add the eggs and oil to the bowl. Beat all the ingredients together until they are well mixed.

You will need:
Extra equipment:
a loaf tin 20 x 13 cm (8 x 5 in.)

Ingredients:
150 g (5 oz) soft brown sugar
2 eggs
150 g (5 oz) self-raising flour
1 teaspoon baking powder
50 g (2 oz) chopped walnuts
50 g (2 oz) raisins
700 g (4 oz) grated carrots
150 ml (¼ pint) oil
For the topping:
75 g (3 oz) cream cheese
1 teaspoon vanilla essence
50 g (2 oz) icing sugar
chopped walnuts to decorate
Preheat the oven to 180°C / 350°F /
gas mark 4

**4** Spoon the mixture into the prepared tin, spreading it into the corners, and smooth the top with a spoon. Bake the cake for one hour, or until it is firm to the touch.

**5** To make the topping, mix the icing sugar, cream cheese and vanilla essence together.

**6** Spread the topping mixture over the cake and sprinkle it with chopped walnuts. Keep the cake in the fridge until you are ready to serve it.

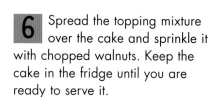

# Sticky Buns

These buns are packed with goodness for you and your friends

# Sticky Buns

**1** Use a paper towel to grease the baking tray with a little vegetable oil. Put the dates and water into a saucepan over a low heat and cook them gently for 5–10 minutes. Remove them from the heat and beat them with a wooden spoon until smooth. Allow them to cool.

You will need:

Extra equipment
a baking tray
grater

Ingredients:
75 g (3 oz) stoned dates
85 ml (3 fl oz) water
85 ml (3 fl oz) orange juice
85 ml (3 fl oz) vegetable oil
225 g (8 oz) self-raising
wholemeal flour
grated rind of 1 lemon

For the topping:
2 tablespoons runny honey
1 tablespoon concentrated
apple juice

Preheat the oven to 180°C / 350°F / gas mark 4

**Take Note!**
Graters are sharp, so take care to mind your fingers!

**2** Put the cooled date mixture into a mixing bowl. Add the orange juice and the oil and mix them together.

**3** Sift the flour into the mixture. Add the grated lemon rind and gently mix it in.

**4** Use your hands to bring the mixture together into a smooth dough. Break the dough into eight or nine small balls, flattening each onto the baking tray with your hand. Bake the buns for 15–20 minutes.

**5** While the buns are in the oven, make the topping. Put the honey, apple juice and water into a saucepan and heat it gently, stirring all the time.

**6** When the buns are cooked, spoon a little of the topping over each one. Leave the buns to cool on the tray.

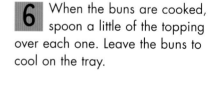

# Gingerbread People

Create your own gingerbread family with this great recipe

# Gingerbread People

**1** Use a paper towel to grease the baking tray with a little margarine. Sift the flour, bicarbonate of soda, ground ginger and ground cinnamon into a mixing bowl.

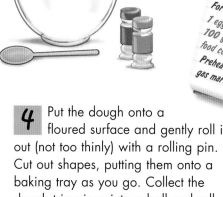

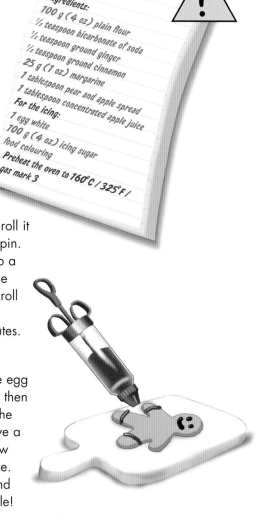

You will need:

Extra equipment:
a baking tray
cookie cutters
an icing syringe

Ingredients:
100 g (4 oz) plain flour
½ teaspoon bicarbonate of soda
½ teaspoon ground ginger
½ teaspoon ground cinnamon
25 g (1 oz) margarine
1 tablespoon pear and apple spread
1 tablespoon concentrated apple juice
For the icing:
1 egg white
100 g (4 oz) icing sugar
food colouring
Preheat the oven to 160°C / 325°F / gas mark 3

**2** Put the margarine, pear and apple spread and concentrated apple juice into the saucepan over a low heat, and stir until melted.

**4** Put the dough onto a floured surface and gently roll it out (not too thinly) with a rolling pin. Cut out shapes, putting them onto a baking tray as you go. Collect the dough trimmings into a ball and roll them out to make more biscuits. Bake in the oven for 10–15 minutes. Cool on a wire rack.

**5** To make the icing, beat the egg white in a small bowl, and then sift the icing sugar on top. Beat the ingredients together until you have a smooth, stiff paste, and add a few drops of food colouring if you like. Spoon the icing into a syringe and decorate your gingerbread people!

**3** Ask an adult to pour the melted margarine mixture onto the flour in the bowl. Mix the ingredients to form a firm dough.

# Chocolate Muffins

These yummy chocolate muffins are great for parties!

# Chocolate Muffins

**1** Grease the muffin tray with a little soft butter.

**2** Put the butter, the sugar, the egg and the flour into a large mixing bowl. Stir them all together with a wooden spoon until they are well mixed.

**3** Sift the baking powder and cocoa powder into the bowl. Add the milk. Mix them together.

You will need:

Extra equipment:
a muffin tray

Ingredients:
50 g (2 oz) butter
75 g (3 oz) brown sugar
1 egg
100 g (4 oz) plain flour
90 ml (3 fl oz) milk
2 teaspoons baking powder
1 tablespoon cocoa powder

Preheat the oven to 190°C / 375°F / gas mark 5

**Top Tip**
To soften the butter, take it out of the fridge at least 30 minutes before cooking.

**4** Use a teaspoon to divide the mixture equally into the muffin tray. Bake the muffins for 12 minutes.

**5** Leave the muffins in the tray until they are cool, and then decorate them with buttercream icing if you want to (see pages 34–35 for ingredients and method).

# Butterfly Buns

These buns may look fancy, but they're simple to make!

# Butterfly Buns

**1** Put the paper bun cases in the bun tray.

You will need:
Extra equipment:
a bun tray
paper bun cases

Ingredients:
100 g (4 oz) butter
100 g (4 oz) granulated sugar
2 eggs
100 g (4 oz) self-raising flour

For the buttercream icing:
75 g (3 oz) butter
150 g (6 oz) icing sugar
1-2 tablespoons milk
food colouring (optional)

Preheat the oven to 190°C / 375°F / gas mark 5

**Top Tip**
To soften the butter, take it out of the fridge at least 30 minutes before cooking.

**2** Put the butter and sugar into a mixing bowl. Use a wooden spoon to beat them together until the mixture is fluffy and very pale in colour.

**4** Sift the rest of the flour into the bowl. Use a tablespoon to mix the ingredients gently, as if you were drawing a figure eight. This will make sure your mixture stays nice and fluffy.

**5** Use a teaspoon to transfer equal amounts of the mixture to the bun cases. Bake the buns for 20–25 minutes or until they are well risen and golden brown. Leave them to cool on a wire rack.

**3** Beat in the eggs, one at a time, adding a tablespoon of flour with each one.

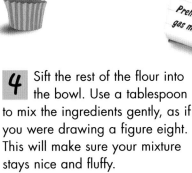

**6** To make the butterfly wings, cut a slice from the top of each cake. Now cut each slice in half.

**7** To make the buttercream icing, use a wooden spoon or an electric mixer to beat the butter in a large bowl until it is soft.

**8** Sift half of the icing sugar into the bowl, and then beat it with the butter until the mixture is smooth. Then sift the rest of the icing sugar into the bowl and add one tablespoon of milk.

**Take Note!**
*Ask an adult to help you use the electric whisk.*

**9** Beat the mixture until it is smooth and creamy. Now add a couple of drops of food colouring if you want to.

**10** If the mixture is too thick, add a little extra milk to make it more runny. Add extra icing sugar if you need to thicken the mixture.

**11** Place a little buttercream icing on top of each bun. Now gently push two of the halved slices into the icing on each bun at an angle to form pretty butterfly wings!

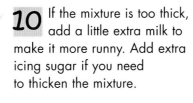

# Colourful Cookies

Let your imagination run wild when you decorate these crazy cookies!

# Colourful Cookies

**1** Use a paper towel to grease the baking trays with a little butter. Put the butter into a bowl, add the sugar, and mix them together until they're light and fluffy.

**2** Add the egg, mixing it in well.

### Top Tip
*Soften the butter by taking it out of the fridge 30 minutes before you need to use it.*

**You will need:**
Extra equipment:
2 baking trays
cookie cutters
an icing syringe

Ingredients:
100 g (4 oz) butter
100 g (4 oz) caster sugar
1 egg
225 g (8 oz) plain flour

To decorate:
coloured icing (see below)
chocolate chips, sugar sprinkles,
coloured sweets and silver balls

Preheat the oven to 180°C / 350°F / gas mark 4

**3** Sift the flour into the bowl. Gently mix in the flour, and then use your hands to knead the mixture into a smooth dough. Wrap the dough in clingfilm and put it in the fridge for fifteen minutes.

To decorate:
| for water icing: | for royal icing: |
| --- | --- |
| 100 g (4 oz) icing sugar | 100 g (4 oz) icing sugar |
| 1-2 tablespoons of hot water | 1 egg white |
| food colouring | food colouring |

**4** Put the dough onto a floured surface, and sprinkle a little flour onto a rolling pin. Roll out the dough (not too thin), and cut out different shapes. Put the biscuits onto a baking tray and bake them for 10 minutes, until they are golden brown. Lift them onto a wire rack to cool.

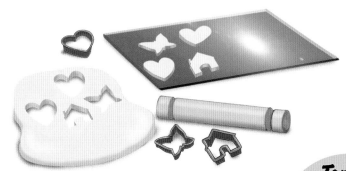

# Decorating the Cookies

**1** Use water icing to cover the cookies. Sift the icing sugar into a bowl and add enough water to make a smooth paste. Add a drop of food colouring if you want to. To make chocolate icing, add one teaspoon of cocoa powder to the icing sugar. Decorate your cookies with sweets or silver balls, or pipe designs with royal icing.

**2** To make royal icing for piping decorations, beat an egg white in a small bowl. Sift the icing sugar into the bowl and beat the mixture until the icing thickens. Add a drop of food colouring if you wish. Spoon the icing into an icing syringe fitted with the nozzle of your choice. Pipe it carefully on to the cookies. Leave it to set.

### Top Tip
Royal icing can be kept for several days in the fridge if you put it into an airtight container.

38

# Ginger Bangs

Give these biscuits a little bang and watch them go crinkly!

# Ginger Bangs

**1** Use a piece of paper towel to lightly grease the baking trays with a little margarine.

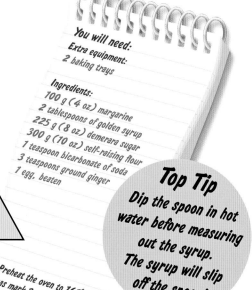

You will need:
Extra equipment:
2 baking trays

Ingredients:
100 g (4 oz) margarine
2 tablespoons of golden syrup
225 g (8 oz) demerara sugar
300 g (10 oz) self-raising flour
1 teaspoon bicarbonate of soda
3 teaspoons ground ginger
1 egg, beaten

Preheat the oven to 160°C / 325°F / gas mark 3

**Top Tip**
Dip the spoon in hot water before measuring out the syrup. The syrup will slip off the spoon!

**2** Put the margarine, golden syrup and demerara sugar into a pan over a medium heat. Stir with a wooden spoon until the margarine has melted. Remove the pan from the heat.

**3** Sift the flour, bicarbonate of soda and ground ginger into a bowl.

**4** Ask an adult to pour the melted margarine mixture into the bowl, and mix it together well. Stir the beaten egg into the rest of the mixture.

**5** Use your hands to make balls of dough about 2.5 cm (1 in.) across. Put them onto the baking trays, leaving plenty of space in between.

**6** Bake the biscuits in the oven for 10–12 minutes. Ask an adult to give the trays a little bang on the work top to make the biscuits go crinkly. Leave the biscuits on the trays for 2–3 minutes, and then transfer them to a wire rack to cool.

# Crunchy Cookies

Munch these tasty Crunchy Cookies as a snack with a drink

# Crunchy Cookies

You will need:

Extra equipment:
a baking tray
a round cookie cutter 5 cm (2 in.)

Ingredients:
100 g (4 oz) soft margarine
75 g (3 oz) demerara sugar
100 g (4 oz) plain wholemeal flour
100 g (4 oz) porridge oats

Preheat the oven to 180°C / 350°F / gas mark 4

**1** Use a paper towel to grease the baking tray with a little soft margarine. Put the margarine and sugar into a bowl and mix them together with a wooden spoon.

**2** Add the flour and the oats to the bowl. Mix everything together, using a spoon and then your hands, to make a soft dough.

**3** Put the dough onto a floured surface and gently press it out.

**4** Cut out circles of dough and put them onto the baking tray.

**5** Bake the cookies in the oven for 12–15 minutes, until they are golden brown. Place the cookies onto a wire rack to cool.

# Choc-chip Cookies

If you love chocolate, you'll love these Choc-chip Cookies!

# Choc-chip Cookies

You will need:
Extra equipment:
a baking sheet

Ingredients:
75 g (3 oz) soft margarine
75 g (3 oz) caster sugar
100 g (4 oz) self-raising flour
2 teaspoons cocoa
120 ml (4 fl oz) milk
50 g (2 oz) chocolate chips

Preheat the oven to 180°C / 350°F / gas mark 4

**1** Use a paper towel to grease the baking tray with a little margarine.

**2** Put the margarine and sugar into a large bowl and mix them together with a wooden spoon until they are light and fluffy.

**3** Sift the flour and cocoa into the bowl. Stir them into the mixture.

**4** Add the milk and the chocolate chips, and mix them all together.

**5** Put 8–10 teaspoons of the mixture onto the greased tray (you will probably have enough mixture for two batches). Bake the cookies for 15–20 minutes. Leave them to cool for 2–3 minutes before lifting them onto a wire rack to cool completely.

44

# Yummy Flapjacks

These yummy flapjacks are packed with oats!

# Yummy Flapjacks

**1** Use a paper towel to grease the tin with a little butter. Put the butter, sugar and honey (or golden syrup) in a pan over a low heat. Stir the ingredients together until the butter has melted and the sugar has dissolved.

**2** Take the pan off the heat and stir in the porridge oats, mixing well. If you are making fruit and nut flapjacks, stir these ingredients in as well.

**You will need:**
Extra equipment:
a baking tin 28 x 18 cm (11 x 7 in.)

**Ingredients:**
225 g (8 oz) butter
75 g (3 oz) sugar
2 tablespoons honey or golden syrup
350 g (12 oz) porridge oats

**For fruit and nut flapjacks:**
100 g (4 oz) sultanas, raisins or currants
50 g (2 oz) chopped nuts

**For chocolate flapjacks:**
100 g (4 oz) plain chocolate

Preheat the oven to 180°C / 350°F / gas mark 4

**Take Note!**
Ask an adult to help you melt the ingredients.

**3** Spread the mixture into the tin, and press it down with the back of a spoon. Bake the flapjacks for 20–25 minutes. Take care not to overcook them or they will taste too dry. Cut the mixture into twelve pieces, and leave them in the tin to cool completely.

## Chocolate Flapjacks:

**1** Ask an adult to help you melt the chocolate in a heatproof bowl over a pan of simmering water (or use a microwave).

**2** Take the bowl off the pan. Dip the ends of each flapjack into the melted chocolate, and leave them to set on a wire rack.

# Christmas Tree Cookies

These clever cookies will make your Christmas tree look really special

# Christmas Tree Cookies

You will need:

Extra equipment:
a baking tray
a clean plastic bag
a skewer
cookie cutters
several metres of fine ribbon
or silver thread

Ingredients:
225 g (8 oz) plain flour
½ teaspoon ground mixed spice
100 g (4 oz) butter
100 g (4 oz) caster sugar
1 tablespoon milk
10 coloured boiled sweets

Preheat the oven to 180°C / 350°F /
gas mark 4

**1** Use a paper towel to grease the baking tray with a little butter. Sift the flour and ground mixed spice into a bowl.

**2** Cut the butter into small pieces. Add it to the flour, and rub the mixture through your fingertips until it looks crumbly.

**3** Add the sugar and milk to the bowl, and knead the mixture into a soft dough. Wrap the dough in clingfilm and put it in the fridge for 15 minutes.

48

**4** Put the dough onto a floured surface and roll it out. Use cookie cutters to cut out different shapes, and put them on the baking tray.

**5** Put the boiled sweets in a plastic bag and crush them with a rolling pin. Carefully cut out a small hole from the centre of each cookie. Fill the holes with the crushed sweets. Use the skewer to pierce a hole in the top of each cookie.

**6** Bake the cookies for 10–15 minutes, until they are golden brown and the sweets have melted. Once the melted sweets have set, carefully lift the cookies onto a wire rack to cool.

**7** Thread the hole at the top of each cookie with ribbon or thread, and hang them on your Christmas tree!

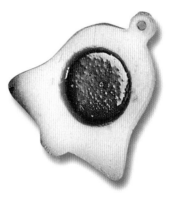

# Chocolate Crunch

This crunchy treat is great to take on a picnic!

# Chocolate Crunch

You will need:

Extra equipment:
a square tin 18 cm (7 in.)
a clean plastic bag

Ingredients:
75 g (3 oz) butter
75 g (3 oz) plain chocolate
2 tablespoons golden syrup
175 g (6 oz) digestive biscuits
75 g (3 oz) raisins
25 g (1 oz) desiccated coconut
50 g (2 oz) chopped nuts

To decorate
25 g (1 oz) plain chocolate
coloured chocolate drops

**1** Use a paper towel to grease the tin with a little butter. Put some water in a saucepan and warm it over a low heat. Put the butter, chocolate and golden syrup into a heatproof bowl. Ask an adult to help you stand the bowl over the pan, stirring the ingredients until they have melted.

### Top Tip
*Dip a spoon in hot water before measuring the syrup – the heat makes the syrup slide off the spoon!*

**2** Put the biscuits into a clean plastic bag and crush them with a rolling pin.

**3** Take the bowl off the pan, and add the biscuits, raisins, coconut and chopped nuts, mixing everything together thoroughly. Put the mixture into the tin, pressing it down firmly.

**4** To decorate, melt the chocolate in a clean bowl over a pan of simmering water, as before. Spread the chocolate evenly over the mixture in the tin. Mark nine squares in the chocolate crunch, and then put the chocolate drops on top. Leave it to set in a cool place for 2–3 hours and then cut it into squares.

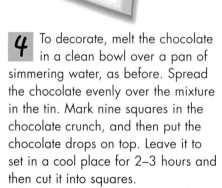

# Marshmallow Fudge Cookies

These cookies are wonderfully sticky and make a delicious treat!

# Marshmallow Fudge Cookies

**You will need:**

Extra equipment:
a square tin 18 cm (7 in.)
a clean plastic bag

Ingredients:
A little vegetable oil
175 g (6 oz) cornflakes
100 g (4 oz) marshmallows
100 g (4 oz) butter
100 g (4 oz) plain fudge

**1** Wipe around the sides and bottom of the baking tin with a little oil on a paper towel. Put the cornflakes into a plastic bag and crush them with a rolling pin.

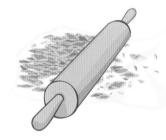

**2** Put the marshmallows, butter and fudge into a saucepan. Ask an adult to help you stir them over a low heat until they've melted.

**3** Take the pan off the heat and add the cornflakes, stirring them until they are covered with the marshmallow mixture.

**4** Spread the mixture into the tin, pressing it down with the back of a spoon. Leave it to set in a cool place for 2–3 hours.

**5** When completely cool, cut the Marshmallow Fudge Cookies into squares.

53

# White Chocolate Cookies

These cookies are so tiny you can eat loads!

# White Chocolate Cookies

You will need:
Extra equipment:
paper bun cases

Ingredients:
225 g (8 oz) white chocolate
25 g (1 oz) butter
225 g (8 oz) chunky fruit
and nut muesli

**1** Put a little water in a saucepan, and put a heatproof bowl over the pan. Break the chocolate into small pieces, and put it into the bowl with the butter. Ask an adult to help you stir the ingredients gently over a low heat until they have melted.

**Top Tip**
These little cookies taste just as good made with milk chocolate!

**2** Take the pan off the heat, and take the bowl off the pan. Add the muesli to the bowl and stir it into the chocolate mixture until it is thoroughly coated.

**3** Spoon a little of the mixture into each paper bun case. Leave the White Chocolate Cookies in a cool place to set.

# Orange Spice Cookies

These cookies are really crisp and light with an orange zing!

# Orange Spice Cookies

**1** Put the butter and sugar into a bowl, and beat them together with a wooden spoon until they are light and creamy.

You will need:

Extra equipment:
2 baking trays

Ingredients:
100 g (4 oz) butter
200 g (7 oz) caster sugar
1 large egg
grated rind of 1 orange
225 g (8 oz) self-raising flour
2 teaspoons ground mixed spice

Preheat the oven to 190°C / 375°F / gas mark 5

**Top Tip**
Soften the butter by taking it out of the fridge 30 minutes before cooking.

**2** Add the egg and orange rind to the bowl, mixing them together well.

**3** Sift the flour and mixed spice into the bowl, and stir them into the butter mixture.

57

**4** Put the dough onto a floured surface and mould into two sausage shapes with your hands (about 5 cm (2 in.) in diameter). Wrap the dough in tin foil and put it into the fridge for three hours.

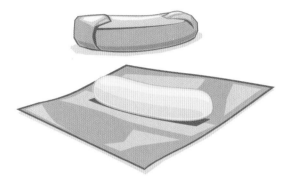

**5** Use a paper towel to grease the baking trays with a little butter.

**Top Tip**
*You can keep any uncooked dough in the fridge for up to two weeks. Every time you want to have some fresh-baked cookies, simply slice some from the roll and bake them in the oven.*

**6** Take one dough sausage from the fridge, unwrap it, and cut off 10–12 thin slices. Place them well apart from each other on the baking trays, and bake them in the oven for 7–9 minutes.

**7** Remove the cookies from the oven, leave them on the trays for a minute or two, and then lift them onto a wire rack to cool.

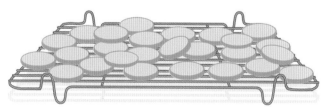

# Mississippi Mud

Here is a recipe for cookies as sticky as Mississippi mud!

# Mississippi Mud

**1** Use a paper towel to lightly grease the baking trays with a little soft butter.

You will need:

Extra equipment:
2 large baking trays

Ingredients:
100 g (4 oz) butter
100 g (4 oz) dark brown sugar
1 egg
a few drops of vanilla essence
100 g (4 oz) plain flour
½ teaspoon of bicarbonate of soda
½ teaspoon of salt
100 g (4 oz) plain chocolate,
finely chopped, or chocolate chips
50 g (2 oz) chopped walnuts

Preheat the oven to 180°C / 350°F /
gas mark 4

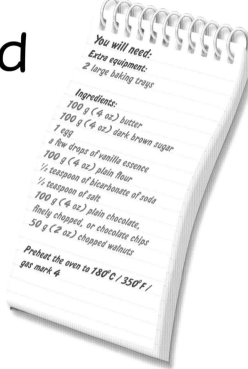

**2** Put the butter and sugar into a bowl, and beat them together with a wooden spoon until light and creamy.

**3** Add the egg and vanilla essence to the bowl, and mix the ingredients together well.

**4** Sift the flour, bicarbonate of soda and salt into the bowl. Stir everything together thoroughly.

**5** Add the chopped chocolate (or chocolate chips) and chopped walnuts, mixing them in well.

**6** Spoon heaps of the mixture onto the baking trays, leaving plenty of space between them because the mixture will spread when it cooks. Bake the cookies for 10–15 minutes.

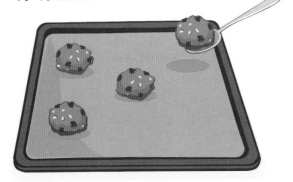

**7** When the cookies are done, remove them from the oven and leave them on the tray for 3–4 minutes. Lift them onto a wire rack to cool completely.

# Peanut Crunch Cookies

You are sure to like these crunchy peanut butter cookies!

# Peanut Crunch Cookies

**1** There is no need to grease the baking trays, just make sure they are clean and dry.

You will need:
Extra equipment:
2 large baking trays

Ingredients:
100 g (4 oz) butter
75 g (3 oz) dark brown sugar
75 g (3 oz) caster sugar
1 egg
150 g (5 oz) plain flour
½ teaspoon bicarbonate of soda
4 heaped tablespoons crunchy peanut butter

Preheat the oven to 180°C / 350°F / gas mark 4

**2** Put the butter and the two types of sugar into a bowl and beat them together with a wooden spoon until the mixture becomes creamy.

**3** Add the egg to the bowl, and mix it in well.

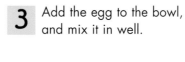

63

**4** Sift the flour and bicarbonate of soda into the bowl. Stir it into the mixture.

**5** Add the peanut butter to the mixture, stirring all the ingredients thoroughly.

**6** Spoon heaps of the mixture onto the baking trays, leaving plenty of space between them. Gently flatten each heap with a fork, to make a pattern on the top. Bake the cookies for 10–15 minutes, checking them regularly to make sure they don't burn.

**7** When the cookies are done, remove them from the oven and leave them on the trays for 3–4 minutes. Then, using the palette knife, carefully lift the cookies onto a wire rack to cool.

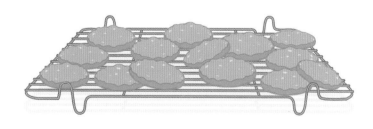

# Super Spicy Energy Bars

These spicy bars will give you enough energy to play for hours!

# Super Spicy Energy Bars

**1** Lightly grease the tin with a little butter and line it with a piece of greaseproof paper.

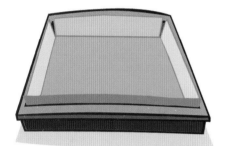

**You will need:**

Extra equipment:
a square tin 18 cm (7 in.)
an icing syringe

Ingredients:
100 g (4 oz) butter
75 g (3 oz) caster sugar
2 eggs
2 tablespoons black treacle
100 g (4 oz) plain flour
1 ½ teaspoons baking powder
1 teaspoon ground cinnamon
1 teaspoon mixed spice
225 g (8 oz) raisins
50 g (2 oz) chopped walnuts

Preheat the oven to 180°C / 350°F / gas mark 4

**2** Put the butter and sugar into a large bowl and beat them together until they are light and creamy.

**3** Beat the eggs together with a fork in a small bowl. Add them to the butter mixture, a little at a time, and mix them in well. Now mix in the treacle.

To decorate:
2 tablespoons icing sugar
2 teaspoons water

**Top Tip**
Dip the spoon in hot water before measuring out the treacle. The treacle will slip off the spoon!

**4** Sift the flour, baking powder, cinnamon and spices into the bowl.

**5** Stir in the raisins and walnuts.

**6** Spoon the mixture into the tin and smooth the top with the back of the spoon. Bake for 15–20 minutes.

  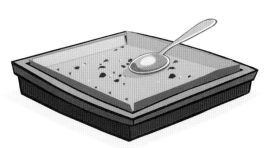

**7** Remove the tin from the oven. When it is cool enough to touch, cut twelve bars from the mixture and transfer them to a wire rack.

**8** You can ice the bars when they are completely cool. Sift the icing sugar into a bowl and add the water, mixing well with a wooden spoon to make a thick paste. Spoon the icing into the icing syringe and decorate the bars with zigzag patterns.

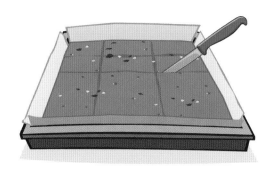

# Lacy Cookies

These cookies become lacy as they cook. Try eating them with ice cream!

# Lacy Cookies

**1** Use a paper towel to grease the baking trays with a little butter. Ask an adult to help you melt the butter in a saucepan over a medium heat. Take the saucepan off the heat and add the sugar and golden syrup.

You will need:

Extra equipment:
2 baking trays

Ingredients:
50 g (2 oz) butter
50 g (2 oz) demerara sugar
50 g (2 oz) plain flour
2 tablespoons golden syrup

Preheat the oven to 180°C / 350°F / gas mark 4

**2** Sift the flour into the pan, and stir it into the melted butter mixture.

**4** Leave the cookies on the trays for 2–3 minutes, and then use a palette knife to lift each cookie onto a wire rack to cool.

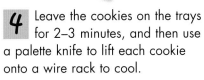

**3** Spoon teaspoons of the dough onto the baking trays. Flatten the top of each with the back of the spoon and bake for 10–12 minutes.

# Lemon Balls

These little lemony balls are soft and chewy inside... yummy!

# Lemon Balls

**1** Use a paper towel to grease the baking tray with a little oil.

**2** Put the ground almonds, sugar and lemon rind into a bowl and mix them together.

**3** Before separating the egg whites from the egg yolks, make sure your hands are very clean! Then break an egg into one hand held over a bowl. Let the egg white drip through your fingers. Put the egg yolk into another bowl, cover and keep in the fridge for another recipe.

**4** Whisk the egg whites with an electric whisk until stiff. Add enough spoonfuls of the whisked egg white to the almond mixture to mix to a stiff paste.

**5** Wet your hands with cold water and roll the paste into small balls. Put the balls onto the baking tray. Bake them in the oven for 10–12 minutes.

**6** Lift them onto a wire rack to cool. Once cool, put them on a plate and sift icing sugar over them until they are completely covered. Serve them in the paper sweet cases.

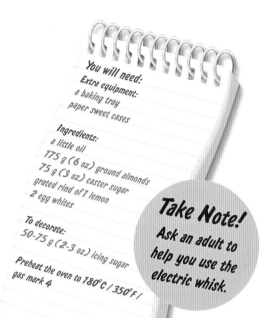

You will need:
Extra equipment:
a baking tray
paper sweet cases

Ingredients:
a little oil
175 g (6 oz) ground almonds
75 g (3 oz) caster sugar
grated rind of 1 lemon
2 egg whites

To decorate:
50–75 g (2–3 oz) icing sugar

Preheat the oven to 180°C / 350°F / gas mark 4

**Take Note!**
Ask an adult to help you use the electric whisk.

# Chocolate Truffles

A box of these chocolate truffles makes the perfect present

# Chocolate Truffles

**1** Ask an adult to put a heatproof bowl over a saucepan of just-simmering water. Make sure the bowl doesn't touch the water. Break the chocolate into small pieces and put them into the bowl, and then add the cream and butter. Stir the mixture until the chocolate has melted.

You will need:

Extra equipment:
paper sweet cases
a plastic container

Ingredients:
150 g (6 oz) plain chocolate
150 ml (5 fl oz) double cream
25 g (1 oz) butter

To coat the truffles:
cocoa powder
chocolate strands
desiccated coconut

### Top Tip
You'll have to roll the truffle balls quickly or the mixture will literally melt in your hands!

**2** Take the saucepan off the heat. Take the bowl off the saucepan and leave it to cool for a few minutes. Carefully pour the melted chocolate into the container. Put the lid on the container and leave it in the fridge to set for 3–4 hours.

**3** Remove the container from the fridge. Roll small balls of the chocolate mixture in your hands.

**4** Roll the chocolate truffles in cocoa, chocolate strands or desiccated coconut, and then put them into the paper cases. Store the truffles in a container in the fridge until you're ready to eat them or give them as a gift.

# Caramelised Nuts

You can keep these gorgeous delicacies in a tin for weeks

# Caramelised Nuts

**1** Put some water in a saucepan and ask an adult to bring it to the boil. Add the nuts, and then turn the heat to low and simmer them for 10 minutes. Drain the nuts into a sieve.

You will need:
Extra equipment:
a large baking tray

Ingredients:
225 g (8 oz) pecan halves, walnut halves or whole blanched almonds
100 g (4 oz) caster sugar
a little oil for frying

Preheat the oven to 150°C / 300°F / gas mark 3

**2** Put the nuts onto a plate and pat them dry with a piece of paper towel. Put them onto the baking tray.

**3** Sprinkle the nuts with the sugar, making sure they are completely covered. Put the tray in the oven for one hour.

**4** Ask an adult to put the oil into the frying pan over a medium heat. Add the nuts and fry them for 2–3 minutes, until the sugar caramelises. When cool, store the nuts in an airtight tin.

# Honeycomb

You can coat honeycomb in melted chocolate or just eat it as it is!

# Honeycomb

**1** Use a paper towel to grease the baking tin with a little butter. Ask an adult to help you put the sugar and syrup into a saucepan over a medium heat. Bring the mixture to the boil, then let it simmer for about 3–4 minutes until the it becomes golden brown.

**You will need:**

Extra equipment:
a square baking tin 18 cm (7 in.)

**Ingredients:**
a little butter
5 tablespoons caster sugar
2 tablespoons golden syrup
1 teaspoon bicarbonate of soda

**For chocolate honeycomb:**
50 g (2 oz) milk chocolate, melted

**2** Take the pan off the heat, add the bicarbonate of soda and mix it in with a wooden spoon. When the mixture froths up, pour it into the baking tin right away.

**Warning!**
The honeycomb mixture will be extremely hot!

**3** When the mixture has cooled, turn it out onto a chopping board and use the wooden spoon to crack it into bite-size pieces.

**4** You can dip pieces of honeycomb into melted chocolate if you like! Leave them to cool on a piece of greaseproof paper.

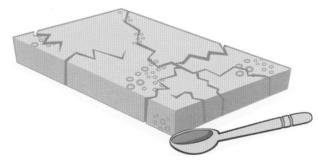

# Peppermint Creams

Coat these icy mints with chocolate for an extra cool kick!

# Peppermint Creams

**1** Sift the icing sugar into a bowl.

**You will need:**

Extra equipment:
none

Ingredients:
450 g (1 lb) icing sugar
1 egg white
a few drops of peppermint essence
food colouring (optional)

For chocolate peppermint creams:
100 g (4 oz) plain chocolate, melted

**Top Tip**
Use food colouring to make different-coloured peppermint creams.

**2** Whisk the egg white in a bowl until it's frothy, then add it to the icing sugar with a few drops of peppermint essence. Mix it together with the wooden spoon to make a very thick paste. Knead the paste with your hands until it is very smooth.

**3** To make coloured peppermint creams, put some of the mixture into another bowl and add one or two drops of food colouring. Mix it well. Do this for every different colour used.

**4** Use your hands to make small balls of paste and flatten them into discs. Put them onto a wire rack to harden slightly.

**5** You could dip your peppermint creams into melted chocolate. Leave them to set on the wire rack.

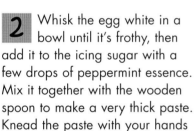

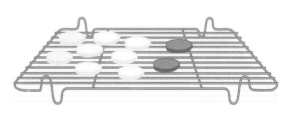

# Coconut Ice

These simple sweets can be made in any colours you like!

# Coconut Ice

**1** Put the tin on the greaseproof paper, and draw around it. Cut out the square of paper large enough to overlap the sides, slit the corners and put it into the tin.

You will need:
Extra equipment:
a square baking tin 18 cm (7 in.)

Ingredients:
900 g (2 lb) caster sugar
150 ml (¼ pt) milk
25 g (1 oz) butter
225 g (8 oz) desiccated coconut
food colouring

**2** Ask an adult to help you put the sugar, butter and milk into a pan over a medium heat, and bring the mixture to the boil. Let the mixture simmer for four minutes, stirring all the time.

**5** Colour the other half of the mixture with a few drops of food colouring. Pour it on top of the mixture in the tin, and leave it to set. Cut the Coconut Ice into squares, but be careful – it will be very crumbly!

**3** Remove the pan from the heat and stir in the coconut.

**4** Ask the adult to pour half the mixture into the tin. Leave it to cool a little.

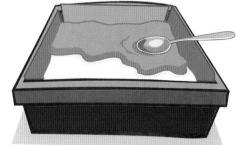

# Almond Sweets

These simple sweets are quick to make and taste delicious!

# Almond Sweets

**1** Put the almonds, sugar and a little orange juice in a bowl. Mix them together to form a stiff paste.

You will need:
Extra equipment:
paper sweet cases
a cocktail stick

Ingredients:
150 g (6 oz) ground almonds
100 g (4 oz) caster sugar
1-2 tablespoons orange juice

To decorate:
icing sugar

For chocolate Almond Sweets:
cocoa powder or
50 g (2 oz) plain chocolate, melted

**2** Use your hands to roll the paste into small balls. To decorate, put a little icing sugar on a plate and roll the balls around in it until they are evenly coated.

**3** For chocolate almond sweets, you can either roll the balls in cocoa powder or cover them with melted chocolate. Use a cocktail stick to dip the almond sweets into the melted chocolate, and then leave them on a piece of greaseproof paper to set.

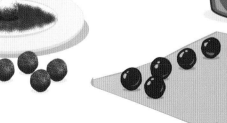

# White Fudge

A wonderful treat for anyone who loves white chocolate!

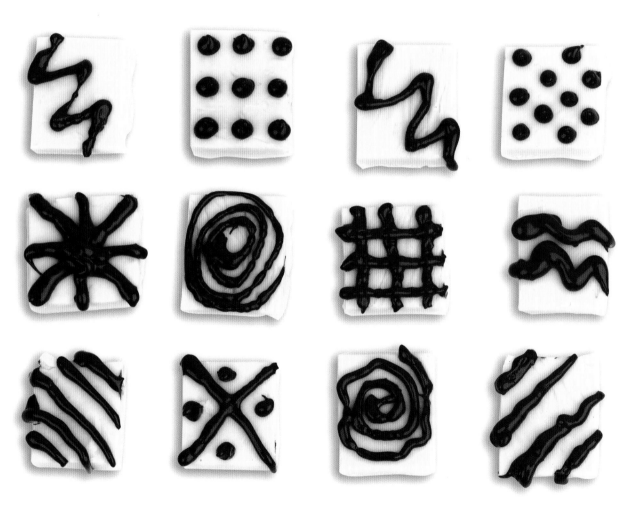

# White Fudge

**1** Line the tin with greaseproof paper. Ask an adult to help you put the chocolate, condensed milk and vanilla essence into a saucepan over a medium heat. Stir them together until the chocolate has melted.

You will need:

Extra equipment:
a square baking tin 15 cm (6 in.)
an icing syringe
paper sweet cases

Ingredients:
300 g (10 oz) white chocolate
200 ml (7 fl oz) sweetened condensed milk
2 teaspoons vanilla essence

To decorate:
50 g (2 oz) plain chocolate

**2** Ask an adult to pour the mixture into the tin, and smooth the top with the back of a metal spoon. Put the tin into the fridge for 3–4 hours.

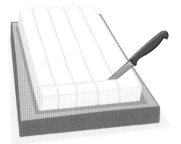

**3** Remove the fudge from the tin by lifting it with the baking paper. Turn it out onto a board and peel off the paper. Cut the slab of fudge into squares.

**4** Put some water into the small pan, put a bowl on top and add the plain chocolate to the bowl. Put the pan on a medium heat and warm it until the chocolate has melted. Put the melted chocolate into an icing syringe and decorate the squares of fudge. When the chocolate has set, put the pieces of fudge into paper sweet cases.

# Chocolate Fruit

Choose your favourite fruits to coat in white and plain chocolate

# Chocolate Fruit

**1** Put the white and plain chocolate in separate heatproof bowls. Ask an adult to help you put some water in a saucepan over a medium heat, and then to place one of the bowls on top (making sure it doesn't touch the water). When the chocolate has melted, take the bowl off the pan, and replace it with the other bowl to melt the rest of chocolate.

You will need:
Extra equipment:
a cocktail stick

Ingredients:
100 g (4 oz) plain chocolate
100 g (4 oz) white chocolate

A selection of fresh fruits to dip:
strawberries
fresh cherries
seedless grapes
pieces of mango
pieces of banana
pieces of pineapple

Alternative dried fruits to dip:
whole, stoned, ready-to-serve
apricots and prunes
glacé cherries

**Top Tip**

Try putting chocolate-coated banana chunks in the freezer for one hour before eating – really delicious!

**2** Meanwhile, prepare the fruit. Leave the stalks on the strawberries and the cherries, and cut the mango, the pineapple and the banana into thick slices. Dip the fruit in the melted chocolate, holding each piece by its stalk or with the cocktail stick, and leave it to set on a piece of greaseproof paper.

## Variation

Try this with dried fruits: whole, stoned, ready-to-serve dried apricots and prunes, and glacé cherries can be dipped in the melted chocolate in the same way as fresh fruit. Dried fruit will keep for longer than fresh fruit dipped in chocolate.

# Chocolate Noisette

Serve these tasty sweets as a treat at the end of a special meal

# Chocolate Noisette

**1** Ask an adult to help you put some water in a saucepan over a medium heat. Put the chocolate and butter in a heatproof bowl on top. Make sure the bowl doesn't touch the water. Melt the chocolate and butter, stirring the mixture with a wooden spoon.

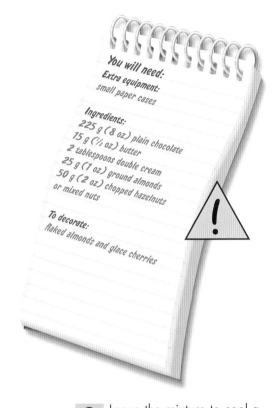

You will need:

Extra equipment:
small paper cases

Ingredients:
225 g (8 oz) plain chocolate
15 g (½ oz) butter
2 tablespoons double cream
25 g (1 oz) ground almonds
50 g (2 oz) chopped hazelnuts
or mixed nuts

To decorate:
flaked almonds and glacé cherries

**2** Remove the pan from the heat and the bowl from the pan. Stir in the cream, ground almonds and chopped nuts.

**3** Leave the mixture to cool a little, and then spoon it into the paper sweet cases. Decorate each Chocolate Noisette with a flaked almond and a glacé cherry, and leave them in a cool place until they have set.

# Easy Turkish Delight

This Turkish delight is sweet and juicy to eat!

# Easy Turkish Delight

**1** Cut the jelly into cubes and put it into a heatproof jug. Ask an adult to boil enough water to cover the jelly up to the 250 ml (8 fl oz) mark. Stir the jelly with a wooden spoon until it has dissolved. Pour the jelly into the dish and put it into the fridge to set.

You will need:
Extra equipment:
a small square dish

Ingredients:
a packet of jelly,
any flavour you like

To decorate:
icing sugar or
desiccated coconut

**Top Tip**
Try pouring a little melted chocolate on top for an even better taste!

**2** When the jelly has set, loosen the edges from the dish, and cut it into squares.

**3** Carefully turn the jelly out onto a plate or board covered in icing sugar or coconut. Turn the squares of jelly until they are completely covered.

# Recipes

Use these pages to write down your own made-up recipes!

# Recipes

# Recipes

# Recipes

# Recipes